Police Dogs

by

Charles and Linda George

Content Consultant:
Officer Don Slavik
St. Paul, Minnesota, K-9 Unit

RiverFront Books
An Imprint of Franklin Watts
A Division of Grolier Publishing
New York   London   Hong Kong   Sydney
Danbury, Connecticut

RiverFront Books
http://publishing.grolier.com
Copyright © 1998 by Capstone Press. All rights reserved.
No part of this book may be reproduced without written permission from
the publisher. The publisher takes no responsibility
for the use of any of the materials or methods
described in this book, nor for the products thereof.
Published simultaneously in Canada.

Printed in the United States of America.

Library of Congress Cataloging-in-Publication Data
George, Charles, 1949-
    Police dogs/by Charles and Linda George.
      p. cm.--(Dogs at work)
    Includes bibliographical references (p. 45) and index.
    Summary: Describes the selection, training, accomplishments, and
history of police dogs.
    ISBN 1-56065-752-9
    1. Police dogs--United States--Juvenile literature. [1. Police dogs.]
I. George, Linda. II. Title. III. Series.
HV8025.G28   1998
363.2'32--dc21

                        97-31740
                          CIP
                          AC

Editorial credits:
Editor, Christy Steele; cover design, James Franklin; photo research,
  Michelle L. Norstad

Photo credits:
Betty Crowell, 10
Michael Green, cover
Image Works/Dorothy Littell Greco, 22, 33
David Macias, 8, 24, 28, 30, 34
Emergency!Stock, 20
Leslie O'Shaughnessy, 6, 19, 27, 37, 43
Photo Network/Mark Sherman, 4, 12
Reynolds Photography, 40
Unicorn Stock Photos/A. Ramey, 14, 38; Deneve Bunde, 16

Table of Contents

About Police Dogs

Police dogs work hard to make the world safer. Some people think police dogs are mean. But this is not true. They are aggressive only on command. Aggressive means fierce.

Police dogs help police officers make sure people obey the law. The dogs find lost people and criminals. Sometimes they chase suspects. A suspect is a person believed to have committed a crime. Police dogs hold the suspects until police officers arrive. Some police dogs locate bombs, drugs, guns, and other illegal objects.

Many police dogs keep going even if they have been injured. They will not stop until they catch suspects or the officers tell them to stop.

Police dogs help officers make sure people obey the law.

Officers praise the dogs when the dogs successfully complete their tasks.

Suspect Identification

Police dogs can help identify suspects. Sometimes a police dog does not catch a suspect. But the police dog can remember the suspect's scent. Police officers may catch the suspect later. Sometimes they put several items of the suspect's clothing in a pile. The clothes have the suspect's scent on them. Police officers make several other piles of clothes. These clothes do not have the suspect's scent.

The dog who chased the suspect smells the piles of clothes. The dog identifies the suspect's scent by barking or sitting next to the pile. A dog's suspect identification cannot be used in a trial.

Handlers and Police Dogs

Police dogs work with trained handlers who are members of police departments. A handler is a police officer who works with a police dog

Police dogs work with trained handlers who are members of police departments.

German trainers felt that German shepherds were among the best dogs for police work.

every day. A police dog usually has one handler. Police train some dogs to work with two or more handlers. These dogs can work even if their usual handlers are sick.

A police dog and its handler must work well together. They become a team. Dogs obey their handlers' commands. They protect handlers in risky situations.

Police dogs live with their handlers. The dogs become members of their handlers' families. At home, they exercise and play together. This builds trust between the officers and the dogs. It also helps them stay in good condition.

First Police Dog Programs

Police officers began working with dogs about 100 years ago. People in Ghent, Belgium, started the first police dog program in 1899. Police officers trained and worked with the dogs. The dogs patrolled with the police officers. Ghent's police dog program was successful in reducing crime. Other cities in Belgium started police dog programs. Soon police departments in other countries started similar police dog programs.

By 1920, special schools in Germany trained police dogs. German trainers experimented with different dog breeds at these schools. The trainers found that German shepherds and Doberman pinschers were the best dogs for police work. These dogs are strong, intelligent, and easy to train.

Today, most major cities have K-9 programs.

First Police Dog Programs in North America

The South Orange, New Jersey, police
department started a police dog program in
1907. The New York City Police Department
started a program in the same year. The dogs
accompanied police officers on patrols. Police
dogs protected police officers and helped catch
criminals. Soon police departments in other
cities started police dog programs.

10

There were problems with most early programs. Dogs ran away, became sick, or fought with each other. Many police departments closed their programs around 1911. Only New York City's program seemed to work. The program continued for 44 years. It ended when patrolling in police cars became popular.

Later Police Dog Programs

In 1956, the Baltimore Police Department started a successful police dog program. The department used only healthy dogs. It had an advanced training program. Police dogs helped officers catch more than 500 criminals during the Baltimore program's first year.

Other police departments heard about the success of Baltimore's K-9 program. K-9 is a short way to spell canine. Canine is another word for dog. K-9 programs use police dogs.

Cities around North America began K-9 programs. Today, most big-city police departments have K-9 programs. There are about 3,000 K-9 programs in North America. Military police also use police dogs.

Best Breeds

Part of a police dog's job is protecting police officers. This is why most police dogs are powerful. People sometimes pick fights with police officers. But they tend to avoid officers who work with police dogs.

Most dogs trained for police work are male. Male dogs are generally larger and stronger than female dogs.

Requirements

Dogs selected for police work should be between one and four years old. Police departments select intelligent dogs that are easy to train. The dogs must be calm and obedient. They must be able to ignore gunfire and other dangers.

Police officers usually choose powerful dogs to become police dogs.

Police dogs must be healthy and strong. The dogs should weigh at least 50 pounds (23 kilograms). They should stand at least 21 inches (53 centimeters) tall at the shoulders.

Many police departments have dogs checked by veterinarians before they become police dogs. A veterinarian is an animal doctor. Veterinarians take x-rays of the dogs' bones. An x-ray is a high-energy beam of light that passes through solid objects. It creates pictures of the insides of objects. The x-ray shows any weaknesses in the dogs' hip bones. Dogs with weak hip bones cannot become police dogs. They are not strong enough for the hard work and long hours required of police dogs.

Skills

Different breeds have different skills. German shepherds, bloodhounds, Labrador retrievers, golden retrievers, Doberman pinschers, and bouviers are excellent tracking dogs. They are

Police dogs must be healthy and strong.

Labrador retrievers were specially bred to be skilled at search and retrieval.

good at following suspects. These dogs can follow a scent many hours after a person has passed through an area.

Labrador retrievers were specially bred to be skilled at search and retrieval. Retrieval means finding an object and bringing it back. These dogs find missing objects.

Many breeds can become police dogs. Doberman pinschers, rottweilers, boxers, Airedales, and giant schnauzers make good police dogs. Bloodhounds are skilled tracking dogs. Bouviers have recently become popular police dogs in California. However, most police dogs are German shepherds, Labrador retrievers, or golden retrievers.

Bloodhounds

Bloodhounds are the best tracking dogs. This breed has an excellent sense of smell. Police use bloodhounds to track and capture suspects and escaped criminals.

Bloodhounds will not quit tracking until they find the source of a scent. They sometimes track until they drop from exhaustion.

Bouvier Dogs

Bouvier dogs came from Europe. Bouvier means cowherd. Early bouvier dogs herded sheep and cattle in Holland, Belgium, and

France. Bouvier dogs have large chests and strong muscles.

Bouvier dogs are intelligent and curious. This makes them good trackers. They are also good at holding on to criminals. Bouvier dogs' jaws can apply 1,500 pounds (675 kilograms) of pressure. A person's hardest bite applies no more than 60 pounds (27 kilograms) of pressure.

German Shepherds

More than 75 percent of all police dogs are German shepherds. These dogs weigh up to 100 pounds (45 kilograms). The sight of a German shepherd stops many criminals from committing crimes.

German shepherds are well-built, powerful dogs. They can work long hours without tiring. Their thick coats are waterproof. They have a keen sense of smell. These qualities make them excellent police dogs.

More than 75 percent of all police dogs are German shepherds.

Police departments sometimes take retrievers in boats to find the bodies of drowned or murdered people.

German shepherds are also quite intelligent. Handlers can train them easily and quickly. The dogs seem to enjoy police work.

Labrador Retrievers and Golden Retrievers

Retrievers are large, powerful, and easily trained. They are able to work in and near water. This can be helpful during police investigations. Retrievers can track suspects through water. They can even smell bodies under water. Officers sometimes take retrievers in boats to find dead bodies. The retrievers hang over the sides of the boats and sniff the water. They alert their handlers when they smell bodies.

Labrador retrievers and golden retrievers also make good detector dogs. Detector dogs locate drugs, bombs, and other illegal objects.

Basic Training

Training teaches police dogs the tasks they will perform while working. It teaches the dogs what to expect from their handlers. Dogs must complete basic training before they can become police dogs. Some dogs do not have the ability to complete police dog training. These dogs are given back to their original owners or placed in good homes.

Dogs learn to obey police officers' commands and follow scents during basic training. Police dogs must follow commands at all times. This helps both the dogs and police officers stay safe.

Dogs must complete basic training before they can take advanced training to become police dogs.

Obedience Training

Police dogs must be obedient. Disobedient dogs could put their handlers, other police officers, suspects, and nearby people in danger.

Dogs must learn basic obedience commands first. Dogs learn to sit, stay, come, stop, and heel. Heel means to walk by a handler's left heel. The dogs learn to obey these commands while they are on leashes. Then the handlers release the dogs from the leashes. Dogs must obey the handlers' commands both on and off the leashes. Those that fail to obey are dropped from the program.

Scent Training

During scent training, police dogs learn to find and follow certain scents. Dogs learn two scenting methods. Sometimes dogs track people or objects by sniffing the ground. Other times, dogs track by air scenting. Air scenting is following a scent in the air. All dogs smell things to learn about their surroundings. But

During scent training, police dogs learn to follow and find certain scents.

handlers teach police dogs to use their scenting abilities on command.

Human beings constantly shed thousands of rafts. A raft is a dead skin cell. Rafts float in the air and smell like the person who shed them. Police dogs find lost people by sniffing the rafts in the air. They learn to follow scents through open fields, woods, and cities. They follow scents into buildings, vehicles, and water. Vehicles include cars, trucks, buses, trains, and airplanes.

A handler hides to teach a dog to follow scents. A trainer instructs the dog to find the handler. The dog is rewarded every time it finds the handler. Handlers reward the dogs by giving toys or treats or by playing games with them.

Next the handler hides farther away or in hard-to-find places. The handler may hide in places full of distractions like food smells. The handler may hide at night. Dogs must learn to find handlers in many situations. Dogs that master these tracking tests learn to track

Handlers sometimes reward dogs by playing games.

other people.

Finally, strangers hide in distant locations. Handlers wait for long periods of time before they send dogs to track the strangers. The scents become weaker as time passes. It is harder for dogs to follow weak scents. The scents become stronger as the dogs get closer to the strangers' hiding places.

Obstacle Course

Police dogs learn to complete obstacle courses. An obstacle course is a series of objects that get in the way. Obstacle courses improve the dogs' agility. Agility is the ability to move quickly and easily.

Dogs climb walls that are 12 feet (almost four meters) high. They walk over thin boards. They climb up ladders and crawl through pipes. The dogs also learn to walk over broken glass and other debris. Debris is the leftover parts of something that has been destroyed. The dogs jump over hurdles. A hurdle is a small fence. Dogs even learn to jump through rings of fire.

Dogs jump over hurdles to complete obstacle courses.

Advanced Training

Police dogs learn special skills in advanced training. They may learn how to apprehend criminals without using too much force. Apprehend means to catch someone. They may learn to identify suspects by scent. Some police dogs learn to find drugs, weapons, or bombs.

Aggression Training

Police dogs must be aggressive on command to be effective on the job. But they must also be able to control their aggression. Dogs learn how to guard, chase, apprehend, and hold on to people in aggression training. Trainers teach dogs to be as gentle as possible during apprehensions.

Police dogs must be aggressive on command.

Some trainers teach dogs to grab and hold suspects' arms. They do this by becoming agitators. Agitators wear pads on their arms. They annoy the dogs by waving sticks or bags.

Handlers keep their dogs on leashes during aggression training. They command their dogs to watch the agitators. Dogs should become alert and watch the agitators closely.

Handlers then give the apprehension command. The dogs should bite the agitators' padded sleeves. Next, handlers give the hold command. The dogs should hold on to the agitators until the handlers give the command to release.

Dogs practice this process many times. They are dropped from the program if they cannot learn to apprehend properly.

Chasing and catching agitators becomes more difficult as training progresses. Agitators hide in buildings. Dogs must search the buildings to find the agitators. They then hold the agitators until their handlers arrive.

Handlers keep the dogs on leashes for aggression training.

Advanced Aggression Training

Police dogs face many risky situations.
Trainers try to prepare dogs for the conditions
they will face on the job. Trainers do this
during advanced aggression training. They test
the dogs in different situations.

Dogs must become used to different sounds
and weapons. Gunfire is a common danger.

During training, agitators fire gunshots. The dogs should ignore the gunshots and obey their handlers' commands. Agitators also use knives, clubs, and other weapons. Police dogs should apprehend agitators despite these weapons. Only skilled police dog trainers should use weapons to train dogs. Police dog trainers know how to handle the weapons safely.

Police dogs also learn to save their handlers. During training, a group of agitators pretends to attack the handlers. The police dogs should apprehend the agitators. They should protect their handlers.

Special Jobs

Some police dogs complete additional training to become detection dogs. The additional training lasts four to 10 weeks. Trainers use scent training to teach the dogs the scents of objects. Some detector dogs learn to find bombs or guns. Other detector dogs learn to find drugs.

Some police dogs complete additional training to become detection dogs.

Bomb detection dogs learn to smell the scents of explosives and other bomb parts. Bomb detection dogs have saved thousands of lives by finding bombs before they explode.

Gun detection dogs learn to smell the explosives used in guns. Gun detection dogs are similar to bomb detection dogs. Most gun detection dogs are also trained to find bombs. These dogs help police officers find guns that have been used to commit crimes.

Drug detection dogs find illegal drugs. They can smell drugs even if the drugs have been wrapped in plastic. Many drug detection dogs work in airports. Drug detection dogs sniff baggage to find the drugs.

Drug detection dogs often sniff baggage to find drugs.

Stories about Police Dogs

Police dogs do important things every day. Sometimes they save their handlers' lives. Other times they find missing children. They find hidden drugs, bombs, and guns. Some track and catch suspects who run away from police officers. They also protect their handlers.

Lexus

The police department in Saint Paul, Minnesota, received a phone call. The caller said police would find drugs in a certain car. The department sent Steve Smith and his K-9 partner Lexus to investigate. Investigate means to gather facts to solve a crime.

Lexus smelled the car. She started barking to indicate that she had found something. Officers searched the car and found 45 pounds

Dogs catch suspects who run away from police officers.

Bloodhounds like this one tracked James Earl Ray after he escaped from prison.

(20 kilograms) of marijuana. Marijuana is an illegal drug.

Sandy and Little Red

In June 1977, James Earl Ray escaped from Brushy Mountain State Prison in Tennessee. James Earl Ray was in prison for killing Martin Luther King Jr.

Police officers brought Sandy and Little Red to the prison. These bloodhounds tracked Ray by his scent. They led police officers to Ray's hiding place in nearby hills. Police officers captured Ray and put him back in prison.

Sauer

Trainers consider bloodhounds the best tracking dogs. But a Doberman pinscher named Sauer has the record for tracking the longest distance.

In 1925, Sauer tracked a criminal 100 miles (160 kilometers) across the desert plains of South Africa.

Farnsworth

In Irvine, California, police officer Steve Frew worked with a bouvier named Farnsworth. Frew nicknamed the dog Farns. On the job, Farns guarded Frew's patrol car. He barked whenever anyone approached the car.

Farns once saved Frew from serious harm. Someone called to report a possible car burglary near a bar. Frew and Farns went to investigate.

Frew drove to the bar. The suspect was in the parking lot. He left Farns in the car and went to talk to the burglary suspect. Twelve men came out of the bar and surrounded Frew and the suspect. These men threatened to hurt Frew if he did not leave the suspect alone.

Farns leaped through the open window of the patrol car. He ran toward the 12 men. He barked at them. The 12 men went away. Frew was not hurt. He arrested the burglary suspect.

Protect and Defend

Police dogs work to make the world a safer place. They have helped capture many criminals who might otherwise have escaped. They search and find drugs, weapons, bombs, and missing persons. Police dogs protect the public from these dangers.

Police dogs work with their human partners for many years. Most dogs stop working when they are eight to 10 years old. Many dogs continue to live with their handlers. Other times, police departments find good homes for the retired dogs.

Police dogs help officers capture many criminals.

air scenting (AIR SEN-ting)—following a scent in the air

handler (HAND-luhr)—a person who works with a dog

heel (HEEL)—a command telling a dog to walk by a handler's left heel

K-9 (KAY-nine)—police dog

obedience training (oh-BEE-dee-uhns TRAY-ning)—teaching an animal to do what it is told

obstacle course (OB-stuh-kuhl KORSS)—a series of objects that get in the way

scent training (SENT TRAY-ning)—teaching a dog to find and follow certain scents

suspect (SUHS-spekt)—a person believed to have committed a crime

TO LEARN MORE

George, Charles, and Linda George. *Bomb Detection Dogs*. Mankato, Minn.: RiverFront Books, 1998.

Patten, Barbara J. *Dogs with a Job*. Read All About Dogs. Vero Beach, Fla.: Rourke, 1996.

Patten, Barbara J. *Hounds on the Trail*. Read All About Dogs Series. Vero Beach, Fla.: Rourke, 1996.

Ring, Elizabeth. *Patrol Dogs*. Brookfield, Conn.: Millbrook Press, 1994.

USEFUL ADDRESSES

Canadian Police Canine Association
8004-4A Street
Calgary, Alberta T2K 5W8
Canada

Dogs Against Drugs/Dogs Against Crime
517 Spring Mill Road
Anderson, IN 46013

K-9 Concepts
406 East Madison
Broussard, LA 70518

United States Police K-9 Association
11780 Beacons Field
Detroit, MI 48224

Washington State Police K-9 Association
Box 1302
Renton, WA 98057

Bo's Nose Knows: The K-9 Unit of the Valparaiso Police Department
http://ww2.netnitco.net/users/perrys/

Police Dog Homepages
http://www.best.com/~policek9/index.htm

The Police K-9 Page
http://www.k9cop.com

Police Resource List—Police Dog/Search and Rescue
http://police.sas.ab.ca/prl/dog.html

United States Police K-9 Association
http://www.minn.net/uspca